THE OLD HOUSE

By Pat Birtwistle

Illustrations by Bradley Moore

Patnor Publishing

ACKNOWLEDGMENTS

A heartfelt thanks to Pat Nelson (my friend and research consultant) for her help and encouragement, Nick Sidoti for his enthusiasm, wealth of ideas and insights; Ann Marie Crocco for allowing the students in her school to pilot these novelettes, Angela Marcov who piloted these novelettes and showed such enthusiasm, and to Carole McGregor and Judy Metler for their editing skills. And a special thanks to Paul Dayboll, Linda Roote and Bradley Moore for their help with how to best get these books printed and for creating our website.

Above all, a very special thanks to Norm, my husband and best friend, for all his hard work in making these books become a reality.

THE OLD HOUSE

By Pat Birtwistle

Illustrations by Bradley Moore

THE OLD HOUSE

CHAPTER 1

The Old House

It was set with big rocks next to it. It looked as if the rocks had trapped it there. The rain and wet fog from the swamp had made the roof and walls black. The door was shut, and the steps were left to rot. No one went to the old house, and the kids looked at it from the swamp. Mom had told the kids that an old man, who had the house, had died in the swamp.

They said that the house was spooky and that crying came from the house. The moms said that the crying was just the wind.

One day, the kids were sitting by the swamp. Kim and Beth wanted to go back to the swamp to look for the hand with the ring. They still wanted to get rich. Dan and Nick wanted to go to the old house.

"We are not to go out there," said Beth. "Why do you want to go to an old house?"

Dan wanted to see if there was a "spook". He just said that for fun. So Dan got the rest of the kids to go with him to the house.

Dan led them to the door. He pushed it. They could see into the room. There were cracks in the walls that let in a little sun. There was not much in the room that he could see.

The kids stepped into the house and stopped. It was spooky, but no one wanted to let on.

The kids could see old stuff in the room. Things smelled musty, and cobwebs hung from the roof. Beth did not want to go in, so she just sat on a stool that was by the door. "We should not be here," she said when the rest of the kids went in. Nick tripped on a boot that he had not seen and he fell with a crash. That made the rats run and Beth yelled.

There were a lot of rats running here and there. Beth could see them and a lot them came running out the door. That spooked Beth and she yelled, "Come on, let's get out of here."

"Shh!" Dan said as he went to one of the rooms. That room was black. There were no cracks in the walls to let in the sun.

Bats hung from the roof of the room. He could not see what was in there. He took a step into the room to have a look, but he still could not see.

"Come in here!" yelled Nick from the next room. When he yelled, the bats swooped. Beth yelled. "Shh!" Kim said. The kids all stopped. At last, the bats went back up to the roof.

Dan and Kim went to see why Nick had yelled. Nick was sitting on an old trunk. There was a lock on the trunk. Kim, Nick and Dan wanted to see what was in the trunk, but they could not get the lock off.

Beth did not go to the room to help. She sat by the door and looked at the bugs as they ran up and down the walls. She felt badly that she did not go with the kids, but she just could not. It was too spooky in there.

"We must go for lunch soon," Beth was thinking. "I do not like it here, and I will not come back." A rat ran past her. That was it! "It is noon," she yelled at the kids. "Let's go for lunch. Just get me back to the block. You can do what you want."

The kids did not want to go for lunch. They wanted to find out what was in the trunk. Nick's Mom had a lot of tools. He had one that could get old locks off. So the kids left the house to go for lunch. As they went, they were thinking of the trunk and what could be in it. They could think of a lot of stuff and what they would do with that stuff. They were thinking of who left the trunk in the house and why they had locked the trunk.

"Nick, get the tools and we will get that lock off. Let's get back fast," Kim said. "We could be rich!"

CHAPTER 2

The Cry

As soon as she had lunch, Kim went to get Beth. The kids had said that they should be at the rock by the swamp at one. When Kim got to Beth's house, Beth's mom said that Beth felt sick and could not come out. Kim did not think that Beth was sick. She wanted to see Beth, but if she did not go, she would not be at the rock by one.

Dan and Nick would go back to the old house. She did not want to be left out. As she went up the block, she met Dan. When they got to the rock, Nick was there with the tools.

"Where's Beth?" asked Nick. "Should we go back and get her?"

Kim told them what Beth's mom had said. They felt badly, but they wanted to get back to the house and find out what was in the trunk.

"Do you think that there could be riches in that trunk?" asked Kim.

"We will soon find out," said Dan.

"It could be just old stuff," Nick said.

"No one would lock up old stuff," said Kim.

As they went into the swamp, it was getting cool. It looked like rain, so they had to be fast.

When they got to the old house, they saw that the door was shut. They did not think that they had shut the door when they left the house.

"Why is the door shut? We did not shut it, did we?" asked Kim.

"The wind could have shut it," said Nick.

"Could be," said Dan. "But let's not go in there too fast."

They pushed the door and looked in. Then they stepped into the room. They looked at the things they had seen. It all looked like it had be-fore, so they went to the room with the trunk. Nick took his mom's tools and got the lock off. The kids got the lid up. They looked into the trunk. There was just old stuff - rags and tools and other stuff like that. They took the stuff out of the trunk, one by one. There could be riches in that mess. The stuff smelled. They did not find a thing that could make them rich.

"Why do you think the old man locked the trunk?" asked Dan.

"He did not want the rats to get his stuff," said Nick. "No one would want it. I think it was all he had. To him, they were his riches."

"It's too bad," said Kim. "I wanted to get rich and...."

Just then, there was a crash from upstairs. The kids stopped. It was still in the house. They went to the door of the room.

"It was just a rat or bat," said Nick.

"It could be just the wind. It is picking up," said Kim as she looked out.

The kids could not see too well. The sun was dim, and the wind was cool. Dan wanted to go upstairs to see what they could find. He did not think that a rat had made that crash. As Kim looked out she said, "It's raining. Look! We should get back. It looks as if it could get bad."

They went to the door and looked out.

The rain was coming down. The wind was up. But, just as they were going to make a run for it, a cry came from upstairs. They stopped. It was like a kid crying. It could just be the wind. They were at the door.

Did a cry come from upstairs? Was it the wind, or was there a spook in the house? They wanted to go up there, but the rain was coming down fast.

"We should get going. What do you think?" Nick asked.

They ran!

Back To The House

The kids could not stop thinking of the crying as they went to bed. The rain kept up. The next day, when the sun came up, the rain stopped. Kim went to find Beth. She wanted to tell her what was in the trunk, and that crying had come from upstairs. Kim wanted Beth to go back to the house with them to find out what was there. Kim did not think Beth would go with them.

When she got to Beth's house, Beth was sitting on the steps. Beth's mom had asked her to get out of the house. Her Mom did not think that she was too sick. So Beth went with Kim.

Kim had seen Dan and Nick on the rocks by the swamp. They got up and went into the swamp just as Kim and Beth got there. They had not seen them coming.

Kim yelled to them, "Come back! Not so fast!"

Nick looked back and saw them.

"Come on," said Kim to Beth. "We will have fun. There is no one at the house, and we could find some stuff that could make us rich. You do not want to see what is out there.

" Oh, you did come at last. We wanted to get going. I could not stop thinking of the crying," Nick said as the kids came into the swamp.

"Do you think it was just the wind?" asked Beth. She did not want them to get mad at her, but she did not want to go into that house.

"It was like a kid crying," said Kim. "But what kid would be at the old house at dusk?"

"Could there be spooks? The old man died and has come back as a spook," Dan said. "But why would he come back?"

"He just had old stuff in the trunk," said Kim. "Or, is there stuff that we did not find yet? That could be it! We should look in all the rooms. We should go upstairs and look there, too. Some of the old man's stuff could be upstairs."

There had been a lot of rain, and so there was a lot of water and mud in the swamp. The swamp was a big mess when it rained. They could not go too fast in all that mud. There were big pools of water, and they had to go from rock to rock to get past them.

As they got to the house, the kids saw mud tracks going up the steps. The tracks led into the house. They had not seen them the day before. They looked up at the door. They had not shut the door when they ran from the house, but the door was shut. Who shut it? Had it been the wind?

The kids went up the steps, and Dan pushed the door. Beth stopped on the steps. She did not want to go in there!

Kim took Beth's hand and led her into the house. The kids could not see too well. As they went in, Nick tripped on some of the stuff in the room. Bats were swooping and rats were running in the room.

"Shh! " Dan said. "Look where you are going."

Softly, the kids went from room to room. The mud tracks led to the steps that went upstairs. The kids did not want to go upstairs yet. They looked in all the rooms. They could see the things that they had seen when they had been here. It all looked as it had the day before. They went back to the steps going upstairs. Dan pushed Nick up the steps. Kim and Beth went to stand by the door. Nick went softly up the steps.

Dan just went up a little. That was when Nick came running down the steps. He grabbed Dan, and they ran for the door.

When they got out of the house, Nick told them that he had seen blood on the top steps. He said that he had felt the spots and that they were wet. He held out his hand. It had blood on it. They all just looked at the blood. That was why the kids had to go back into the house. They had to find out who was in there.

CHAPTER 4

Blood Tracks

The kids sat out on a rock in the swamp, thinking of what they should do. Should they go back in, go for help, or just get out of there?

"Let's get out of here," said Beth. "It could be a man in there."

"We can't just go. What if a kid is trapped? That kid could die if we do not help," Nick said.

"No kid would be in that house," said Beth.

"We have to go back in, Beth," Dan said.

They came up with a plan. Beth would be by the door. She could run for help if things got out of hand. Kim would stand on the steps going upstairs. Dan and Nick would go up and look. They could tell Kim what they saw, and she could tell Beth.

At last, they went back into the house. Beth sat on the stool by the door. Dan, Nick and Kim went upstairs. Kim stopped on the steps and Dan and Nick went on up.

When they got to the top step, they looked at the spots of blood. The track of blood spots led to a room. The door to the room was shut. The cracks in the walls upstairs were little, so they could not see too well. When they got to the door of the room, they did not want to go in.

"What if there is a man in there who does not like kids? What do you think? Should we go in?" asked Nick.

"If we do not go in, we will not find out who was crying, or if it was the wind," said Dan.

"OK," said Nick softly. "Let's do it!"

They pushed the door a little and saw the drops of blood. The tracks led to the end of the room. Dan looked in and saw rags that looked like they had been made into a bed. Nick and Dan stepped into the room. There was not a lot of sun coming into the room, so they had to go in to look. There was no one there. They went to look at the bed of rags. There was blood on the rags.

"We should tell Kim and Beth," Nick said.

"I do not like the looks of this at all," said Dan. "But we should tell them."

As they left the room, they saw little drops of blood that led to the next room. The door to that room was shut too. They would just have to come back up. They went down the steps and led Kim and Beth out of the house.

"The rags looked like a bed," said Nick. "If a kid is in the house, we cannot let the kid die. We have to go back in and find out."

"What if it's not a kid? We should not be here," Beth said.

"A man would not be crying," said Dan.

"The crying could have been the wind," Kim said. "What do you think, Nick? Do you think we should just get out of here?"

"Beth, we must go back in there," said Nick.

"But what if it is NOT a kid?" asked Dan.

"Let's not go back in there," said Beth. "Let's go!"

The kids did not want to think of who was in the house, if it was not a kid. But they kept thinking of the crying and the tracks of blood.

Beth did not like the plan at all. She was thinking that she should not have come out here with the kids. The moms and dads had said that they should not be in the swamp. The kids were in the swamp, AND at the old house. The moms and dads would get mad, and Beth did not want that.

At last, they went back into the house. One by one they went softly upstairs. They went into the room where the rags were. Kim ran into the wall and ... "crash"!

The crash spooked the bats and they swooped here and there. When the bats went back to the roof, the kids left the room.

"Look where you are going, Kim," Nick said. "You are not helping things."

"I can't see too well up here," said Kim.

They went to the door of the next room. Dan pushed the door just a crack. A cool wind came from the room. He pushed it so they could see into the room. It was too black to see what was in there.

Dan stepped into the room to take a look. When he stopped, Nick pushed past him. He could tell that Dan had seen who was in the room. Kim and Beth could not see. It was like looking into a black pool, so they had to go in.

"What is it?" asked Kim.

Then the kids all stopped and looked at a spot next to the wall.

CHAPTER 5

Do Not Go Into The Swamp

In the room, the kids could see who it was
that had been crying. They saw who had made the
tracks of blood. Kim stepped past Nick and Dan.
She went into the room. There, sitting on a stool,
was a little kid. He did not get up. Kim went and sat
next to him. Kim took his little hand, and the kids
led him out of the house.

"Who are you?" Beth asked. "Are you lost?"

"Why were you in the old house?" asked Nick.

"Do you want food?" asked Kim.

"Are you cut? Let me see that cut," said Beth.

The kids could not think of why the little kid would be in the house by the swamp. They sat on the steps and looked at him. He was little and thin. At last he said, "I am Ted and I want my mom and dad. I want food."

They took Ted to Beth's house. They told Beth's mom what they did. Beth's mom was a cop, and she could help them find Ted's mom and dad.

Beth got food for Ted as Nick and Dan ran to find Beth's mom. When they did find her, he could tell they were upset.

When she saw them, she was thinking, "What did the kids do? I can tell by looking at them that they are in a mess."

"What did you kids do?" she asked.

Before Beth's mom could get mad, Dan jumped in fast.

"We went to the old house by the swamp," Dan said.

"Ted was in the old house. We could not find his mom and dad," said Nick. "He wanted food. We took him to your house. He has a cut on his hand. We had not seen him before. We could not think of where his mom and dad could be. That is why we came to get you."

"Stop! Stop!" said Beth's mom. "Back up. Who is Ted? Why was he at the old house? Why would a kid be out there? Kids are not to be in the swamp or at that house. It cannot be the kid the cops are looking for. That kid's house is at the back of the swamp. So who is he?"

They went to Beth's house. Beth's mom met Ted and helped with the cut on his hand. She told the kids that the cops were looking for Ted.

" This IS the kid we've been looking for. The cops kept looking in the swamp down at the end. They did not think that he could get past the big hills of rocks and all that water in the swamp."

Like the rest of the kids, Ted was told "not to go into the swamp." The day before, when Dan and the kids went into the swamp up here, Ted went into the swamp by his house.

That was when he got lost. He ran here and there, but he could not find his house. It was raining when he saw the old house. It was dusk and getting cool. He got the old rags and made a bed.

When the sun came out, he went to look for food. He cut his hand. He felt sick and went back to his bed. It was black in that room, so he went to the next room and shut the door. That was when Nick and the kids had come to the house and had seen the tracks of blood. When Ted was upstairs, there was the crash. Ted wanted to get out of there, he said, but he had nowhere to run. Then the kids came and got him.

All the kids went with Ted and Beth's mom to Ted's house.

When they got there, Ted's mom and dad were crying. They ran and hugged Ted. Then, they hugged Beth's mom, then Nick and Dan, then Kim and Beth.

As they left, Ted said softly, "I will not go back into the swamp, Mom."

Beth's mom looked at the kids and asked, "And just why were you kids in the swamp? Why were you at that old house?"

"Well . . . Uh . . . We . . . Uh.. " said Dan.

"Oh, oh!" Beth said.

NEW START SUSPENSE SERIES
BY PATRICIA BIRTWISTLE

THE SWAMP

THE OLD HOUSE

WHAT A DAY

THE JUNKYARD

THE TRIP

AT THE MALL

www.ingramcontent.com/pod-product-compliance
Lightning Source LLC
Chambersburg PA
CBHW060949050426

42337CB00052B/3353